Table of Contents

Introducing Cock

Hot Chongqing Cock

   Instructions

Boneless Chili Cock

   Instructions

Sriracha Honey Cock

   Instructions

Coca Cola Cock

Orange Cock

   Instructions

Black Cock

   Instructions

Cock with Black Beans

   Instructions

Steamed Cock with the Works

   Instructions

   THANK YOU

Hot Chongqing Cock

Prep time

35 mins

Cook time

10 mins

Total time

45 mins

Serves: 4 servings

Ingredients

For the Chicken Marinade

- 3 boneless skinless chicken thighs (cut to bite size pieces)
- 1 teaspoon cornstarch
- ¾ teaspoon salt
- 1 teaspoon cooking oil
- 2 teaspoons Shaoxing wine
- 1 teaspoon dark soy sauce (preference is Kikkoman)

For the Rest of the Dish

- 3 tablespoons oil
- 2 tablespoons Sichuan peppercorns
- 2 slices ginger, julienned
- 5 cloves garlic, sliced
- 1 cup whole dried red chilies
- 1 teaspoon Shaoxing wine
- ½ teaspoon sugar
- 1 scallion, chopped

Instructions

1. Rinse the chicken and add to a bowl and toss with the marinade ingredients. Set aside for 30 minutes.

2. Heat 3 tablespoons oil in a Chinese wok over high heat. Add a layer of chicken to the wok and let it sear (DO NOT STIR). Once you have got a good, brown crisp on the bottom of the chicken, stir and continue to sear the chicken until it is browned on all sides. Once the searing is done remove the chicken onto a plate and set aside. Remember with wok cooking you need to make sure your wok is very hot.

3. With the left over oil in the wok turn your heat to medium low and add the Sichuan peppercorns and toast for 2 minutes. Add ginger, garlic and the whole dried chilies and cook for 3 minutes. Watch your heat levels to avoid burning.

4. Now you can add your chicken, Shaoxing wine, sugar, and scallion and stir-fry on high until the liquid in wok has evaporated. Serve with rice or noodles.

Boneless Chili Cock

Prep time
30 mins
Cook time
10-15 mins
Total time
40-45 mins

Serves: 2 servings

Ingredients

- Oil for stir-fry
- 350 gm boneless chicken, diced
- 1 egg, slightly beaten
- ½ cup corn flour
- ½ teaspoon garlic paste
- ½ teaspoon ginger paste
- 1 tablespoon salt or to taste
- 2 cups onions, thickly sliced
- 2 tsp green chilies, thickly sliced (remove seeds if too hot)
- 1 tablespoon soy sauce (adjust according to strength)
- 2 tablespoon vinegar
- Green chilies, slit, for garnish

Instructions

1. Mix the chicken, 2 teaspoon salt, egg, corn-flour, ginger and garlic paste. Make sure the chicken is coated in the batter and leave overnight to marinate.

2. Heat oil in a wok or a pan and stir-fry the chicken pieces over high heat to begin with then lower the heat to medium. Stir-fry until the chicken is cooked through. Drain on absorbent paper.

3. Heat the 2 tablespoon of oil in a Chinese wok and add onions and stir-fry on high heat until they are tender then add the green chilies and sauté for a minute.

4. Now add salt, soy sauce, vinegar and add your chicken back in and stir well for another 2 minutes.

5. Serve hot with the green chilies.

Sriracha Honey Cock

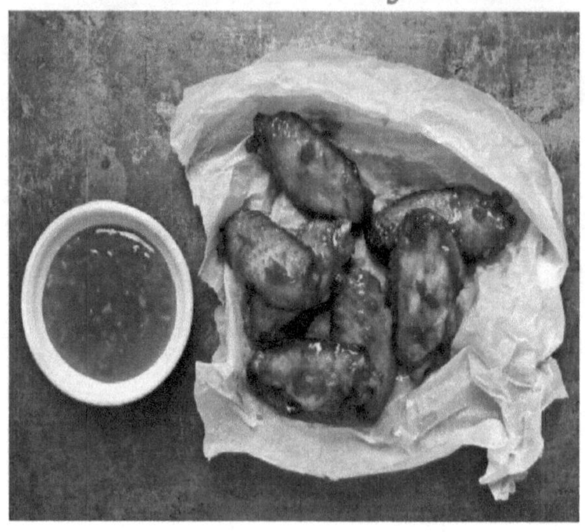

Prep time

5 mins

Cook time

55 mins

Total time

1 hour

Serving size: Serves 4

Ingredients

- 3 pounds chicken wings
- Salt and pepper
- 1 tablespoon oil
- 3 tablespoons butter
- ¼ cup Sriracha Sauce
- 2 tablespoons honey
- 1 tablespoon Shaoxing wine
- 1 teaspoon soy sauce (preference is Kikkoman)
- 1 teaspoon hoisin sauce
- ½ teaspoon salt
- 2 tablespoons chopped cilantro

Instructions

1. Preheat oven to 400 degrees F.

2. Toss the wings with salt, pepper and oil in a large glass bowl.

3. Line a baking sheet with parchment paper, and evenly layout the wings. Set timer and bake for 50 minutes, turning the wings halfway through. The last 2 minutes turn on your broiler to crisp the wings. Watch it carefully.

4. When the wings are almost done melt the butter in a Chinese wok and add Sriracha, rice wine, honey, soy sauce, hoisin, and salt. Stir over low heat until mixed.

5. Take wings out of the oven and toss it in the sauce and add chopped cilantro and serve.

Coca Cola Cock

Prep time

15 mins

Cook time

25 mins

Total time

40 mins

Serves: 6-8 servings

Ingredients

- 2 pounds chicken wings
- 2 tablespoons oil
- 3 slices ginger
- 1 can of cola
- 1 tablespoon Shaoxing wine
- 3 tablespoon dark soy sauce (preference is Kikkoman)
- Salt to taste

Instructions

1. Wash and clean the chicken wings and pat the chicken wings dry with a paper towel.

2. Warm up your Chinese wok on high heat and add the oil, and coat your wok. Add the chicken wings and ginger making a layer around your wok and let it lightly brown on all sides.

3. Once all sides are browned add the Shaoxing wine first then the coca cola, dark soy sauce and bring it to a boil and cover with lid for a minute. Turn down heat to medium and simmer for 15 minutes until the sauce is almost dry. Stir wings and add salt to taste

4. Turn heat back up and quickly stir wings to coat it with the sauce. Serve hot with an ice cold coke.

Orange Cock

Prep time

30 mins

Cook time

10 mins

Total time

40 mins

Serves: 4 servings

Ingredients

For the Chicken

- 1 pound boneless chicken thighs, cut into chunks
- ¼ teaspoon sesame oil
- ⅛ teaspoon white pepper
- ¼ teaspoon salt
- 1 teaspoon Shaoxing wine
- ¼ cup cornstarch
- 1 ½ cup vegetable oil for shallow frying the chicken

For the Sauce

- 1 tablespoon vegetable oil
- 6 dried red chili peppers
- 2 star anise
- ¼ cup fresh orange juice
- ¼ cup chicken stock
- 2 tablespoons rice wine vinegar
- 2 tablespoons sugar
- 1 tablespoon soy sauce
- 2 tablespoons cornstarch, mixed with 2 tablespoons cold water
- 1 scallion sliced on an angle

Instructions

1. Mix your chicken with white pepper, salt, sesame oil and Shaoxing wine.

2. Marinate for 20 minutes. Put the cornstarch in a small bowl and heat the oil in a small pot until it reaches 350 degrees F. Coat the chicken pieces in cornstarch and deep-fry until golden brown. Transfer to a plate lined with paper towels to soak up excess oil.

3. Over medium heat, warm up your Chinese wok and add a tablespoon of oil. Add the dried chili peppers and star anise, and toast for 20 seconds. Add the orange juice, chicken stock, vinegar, sugar, and soy sauce.

4. Simmer the sauce and gradually add the cornstarch mixture, stirring constantly. When the sauce is thick enough to coat a spoon, add the fried chicken and scallions. Toss quickly, and serve with rice or noodles.

Black Cock

Prep time

15 mins

Cook time

1 hour 30 mins

Total time

1 hour 45 mins

Serves: 6 servings

Ingredients

- 1 whole chicken, about 4 pounds (preferably free-range, never frozen)
- 2 teaspoons oil
- 7 slices ginger
- 2 scallions, cut into 3-inch pieces and smashed flat
- 3 whole star anise
- 1 ½ Shaoxing wine
- 3 cups dark soy sauce (preference is Kikkoman)
- 1 cup sugar, plus 2 tablespoons
- 2 teaspoons salt
- 10 cups water

Instructions

1. Thoroughly clean your chicken and remove all the innards.

2. Use a large stock pot – big enough to submerge your chicken with enough of the cooking liquid. Warm up your pot over medium low heat, and add oil and ginger.

3. Caramelize the ginger for about 30 seconds, then add the scallions and cook another 30 seconds.

4. Add the rice wine and star anise and simmer to reduce the alcohol. Add the soy sauce, sugar, salt, and water. Bring to a simmer again and cook on low heat for 20 minutes.

5. After 20 minutes bring the soy liquid to a slow boil and lower your chicken into the soup pot make sure it's submerged in the sauce.

6. Let the chicken cook in the sauce for 5 minutes then turn heat to a low simmer and let it simmer for about 25 minutes.

7. Then turn off the heat, cover the pot, and let the chicken sit in the pot for another 15 minutes.

8. Use meat thermometer to check if your chicken is cooked, it not simmer at low for another 15 minutes. The thickest part should reached 165 degrees F.

9. Once cooked, transfer chicken to cutting board and carve.

10. Serve with rice or noodles. You can freeze the left over sauce and use it for other cock recipes.

Cock with Black Beans

Prep time

35 mins

Cook time

10 mins

Total time

45 mins

Serves: 4 servings

Ingredients

For the Marinade

- 2 medium chicken thighs, cut into bite size pieces
- 3 tablespoons water
- 3 teaspoons cornstarch
- 1 teaspoon oil
- 3 teaspoons soy sauce (preference is Kikkoman)

For the Rest of the Dish

- ½ teaspoon sugar
- Salt to taste
- 1 tablespoon Shaoxing wine
- 2 tablespoons water
- 3 tablespoons oil, divided
- 3 slices ginger, julienned
- 3 cloves garlic, smashed and chopped
- 3 scallions, chopped and separated into white and green parts
- 3 tablespoons fermented black beans sauce
- 1 green bell pepper, cut into bite-sized pieces
- 1 red bell pepper, cut into bite-sized pieces

Instructions

1. Combine the marinade ingredients in a bowl and mix with the chicken. Allow to marinate for 30 minutes.

2. Heat your Chinese wok over high heat and coat your wok with 2 tablespoons of oil. Add the chicken, and quickly spread the pieces into a single layer and cook for 3 minutes on both sides. Once cooked transfer the chicken to a dish and set aside.

3. Over medium heat add 1 tablespoon of oil into the wok. Add ginger, garlic, the white parts of the scallions, and the black beans sauce and cook it for about a minute then heat to high. Add the green and red peppers, and stir-fry for about another minute then add the sugar, Shaoxing wine, salt, the chicken, 2 tablespoons of water, and the green parts of the scallion.

4. Stir-fry everything in the wok until its well coated in the sauce. Plate and serve with rice or noodles.

Steamed Cock with the Works

Prep time

Over Night

Cook time

15 mins

Total time

30 mins

Serves: 4 servings

Ingredients

- ¼ cup dried wood-ear mushrooms
- ⅓ cup dried lily flowers
- 10 medium dried shiitake mushrooms, soaked until soft
- 1 pound boneless chicken thighs, cut into large bite-sized chunks
- ¼ cup water
- 1 tablespoon vegetable oil
- ¼ teaspoon sesame oil
- 1 tablespoon Shaoxing wine
- 1 tablespoon oyster sauce
- ¼ teaspoon sugar
- ¾ teaspoon salt
- ¼ teaspoon freshly ground white pepper
- ½ teaspoon grated ginger
- 1 scallion, chopped (white and green portions divided)
- 1 tablespoon cornstarch

Instructions

1. Rinse the following dry ingredients thoroughly: wood-ear mushrooms, dried lily flowers shiitake mushrooms.

2. Soak the wood-ear, lily flowers and shiitake mushrooms in three separate bowls – soak overnight

3. Once the dry ingredients are hydrated squeeze the excess water from all three ingredients and roughly chop everything up.

4. In a mixing bowl add the cut chicken pieces and the rest of the ingredients into a mixing bowl. Add vegetable oil, sesame oil, Shaoxing wine, oyster sauce, sugar, salt, white pepper, grated ginger, and the white portions of the scallions and mix well and let it marinate overnight (save the green portions of the scallions for the next day)

Please Note: Steps 1 through 4 should be done the night before. When you are ready to cook follows Steps 5 through 7.

5. When you're ready to cook let the chicken mixture come to room temperature and add cornstarch into the mixture and mix well.

6. Transfer the chicken mixture to a deep dish – and place in a covered steamer and steam over medium heat for 10 minutes then shut off heat and let it rest for 2 minutes in the steamer.

7. Remove the dish and garnish with the green scallions and serve with rice or noodles.